Dedicated to Our Four Littles

This book is dedicated to the four littles who brighten our world in every way. **Micah, Kinzie, Luna, and Serenity** — being chosen by God to be your parents is one of our greatest blessings. Each of you adds a unique and beautiful leaf to our family shrub, making it whole and full of life. May you always lean on the Lord, trusting Him for guidance, strength, and nourishment in every season ahead.

With all our love, always,
Mommy Ashley & Daddy Andrew

Text copyright © 2025 by Ashley Rae Klinger. All rights reserved. Illustrated by QBN Studios. No part of this publication, including its concept and characters, may be reproduced, distributed, or transmitted in any form or by any means, including photocopying, recording, other electronic or mechanical methods, or by information storage and retrieval system, without prior written permission of the author and publisher, except in the case of brief quotations embodied in reviews and certain other non-commercial uses permitted by copyright law. The concept of The Great Debate was uniquely created and is the intellectual property of Ashley Rae Klinger and It's Her Brand Enterprises.

Message Mission

With a passion for crafting meaningful messages and building life-changing platforms—and for sharing those messages with audiences around the world—author Ashley Rae (Klinger) introduced **A Shrub Not a Tree** in 2023 as the first book in a special collection of children's stories inspired by her family's growth and their journey through infertility, adoption, and foster care. **The Great Debate** is the second book released in that collection.

Each book is intentionally designed with a dual-layered message. The first part speaks directly to children of all ages, offering a thought-provoking, age-appropriate lesson that is simple to grasp. The second part provides adults with deeper insight, unpacking the heart, mindset, and purpose behind the story. The goal is to empower and equip families to spark meaningful conversations — whether the message applies to their own experiences or to the journey of someone they know — and to encourage them to live purposeful, intentional, engaged, and faith-driven lives, both individually and together.

 AshleyRaeKlinger.com, AShrubNotATree.com, ItsTheGreatDebate.com

 @AshleyRae   @AshleyRaeKlinger   @AshleyRaeKlinger

As the sun began to set and the moon rose high in the sky, the Klinger kids were tucked in and ready for bed - eager for tomorrow to begin. "I'm so excited for our BIG day!" exclaimed Luna. "Me too," agreed Serenity. "Let's fall asleep fast so morning comes sooner," added Kinzie.

As the girls snuggled into their beds and fell fast asleep, their older brother Micah lay wide awake, smiling as he thought about all the fun things planned for their very special day. The excitement made it hard for him to close his eyes.

Early the next morning, Kinzie's eyes popped open. She stretched her arms and gasped - TODAY WAS THE DAY! Their very special day was finally here! Overcome by the anticipation, she couldn't wait any longer to get the day started. "Luna, Serenity!" Kinzie whispered with excitement. "Wake up! Today is the day!"

As Luna and Serenity blinked awake, they too remembered what day it was. In an instant, all three were out of bed and buzzing with excitement. "Let's get dressed!" exclaimed Serenity. "Mom set out our special outfits for today," she added. "We better brush our teeth," said Kinzie. "And don't forget to comb our hair," Luna reminded them with a smile.

The girls got ready as quickly as they could and then hurried to the kitchen where their Mom and Dad were making a very special breakfast. But to their surprise, someone was missing. "Where's Micah?" asked Luna. "I think he's getting ready," Mom answered. "We'll eat as soon as he joins us," Dad assured them.

Unable to contain their excitement for the day ahead, the girls grew impatient. Finally, Serenity called out, "Micah, get up!" "I'm up," came his calm voice from down the hall. "Then brush your teeth and comb your hair!" Luna shouted with frustration. "I already did," he replied. "Then hurry up and get dressed!" Kinzie yelled. "I'm dressed," he answered, still calm.

Confused as to why Micah wasn't joining them for breakfast, the girls dashed to his bedroom to see what was taking so long. To their surprise, Micah was...**MAKING HIS BED**!

"Hurry up, we don't have time for this!" cried Serenity. "We need to eat so we can go!"
"Yeah, come on!" pleaded Luna. "It's not important. You can do it later," she added.
"You're just wasting your time," said Kinzie. "It's going to get messy again tonight anyway!"

But Micah didn't rush. He carefully smoothed his blanket, fluffed his pillow, placed his stuffed dog Tuffy on top, and turned to them with a smile. "Did any of YOU make YOUR bed?" he asked. "We don't have time to debate this right now!" exclaimed Serenity. "Yeah, we need to get going," added Luna. "Come on, let's go!"

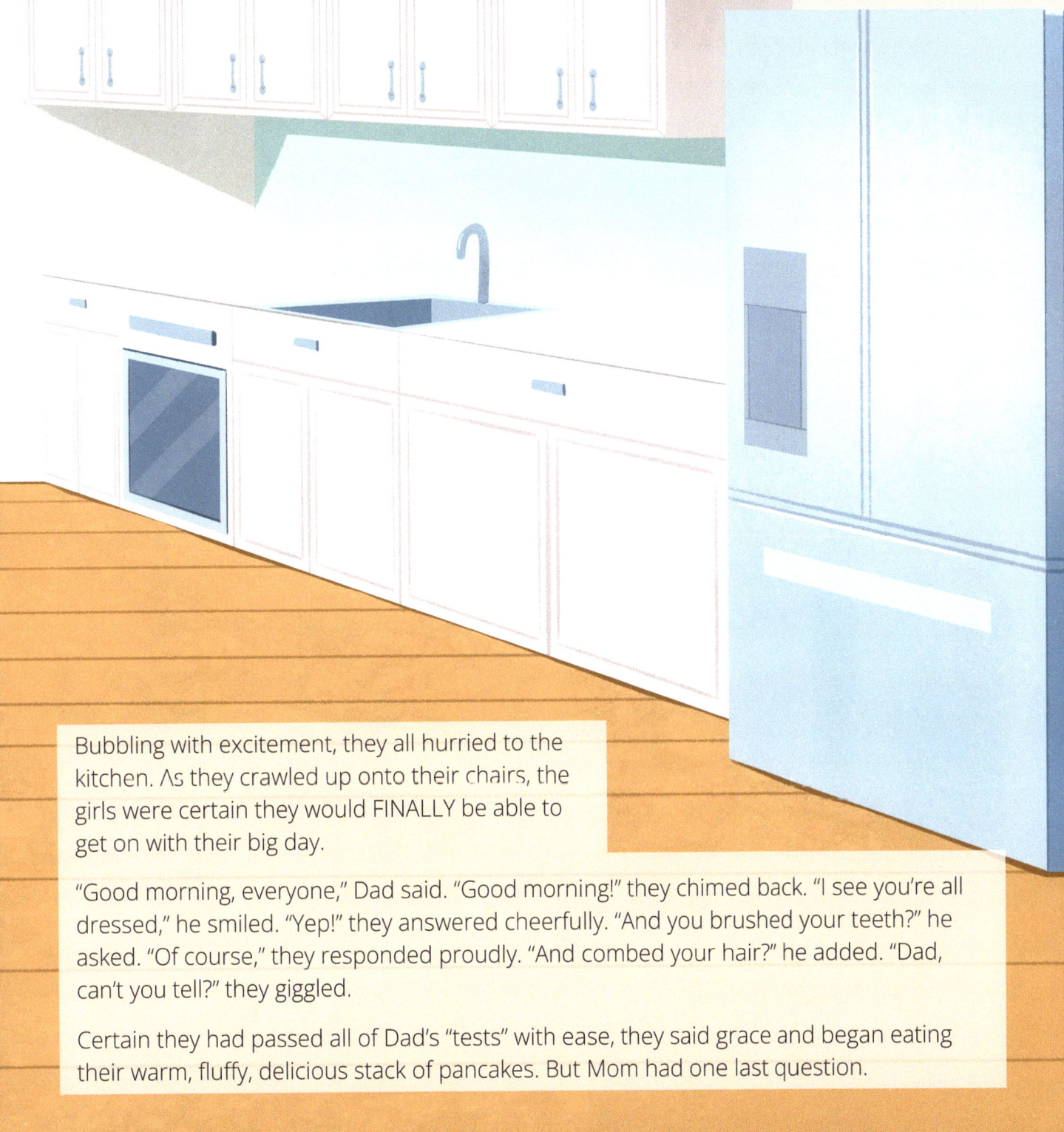

Bubbling with excitement, they all hurried to the kitchen. As they crawled up onto their chairs, the girls were certain they would FINALLY be able to get on with their big day.

"Good morning, everyone," Dad said. "Good morning!" they chimed back. "I see you're all dressed," he smiled. "Yep!" they answered cheerfully. "And you brushed your teeth?" he asked. "Of course," they responded proudly. "And combed your hair?" he added. "Dad, can't you tell?" they giggled.

Certain they had passed all of Dad's "tests" with ease, they said grace and began eating their warm, fluffy, delicious stack of pancakes. But Mom had one last question.

"You all did such a great job getting ready for our big day," Mom began. "Thanks!" they answered cheerfully between bites. "And did everyone make their bed this morning?" she asked. "I sure did!" said Micah confidently with a grin. But the girls said nothing and sat quietly in their chairs.

"Girls?" Mom asked gently. "Did any of you make your beds?" "No…" they mumbled. "Why not?" she asked. "Can't we do it later?" Serenity protested. "Yeah, we just want to go," Luna added. "Ladies, you know we always make our beds at the start of each day," Mom reminded them. "We know," Kinzie said, "but why? They're just going to get messed up again tonight," she insisted. Mom smiled softly. "Come with me, girls," she said.

Back in their room, Mom picked up a pillow from the floor. "Girls, why do you think we want you to make your beds each morning?" "Because it's one of our chores," said Serenity. "Yes, but why else?" Mom asked. "Because it's respectful," Luna added. "True," Mom agreed, "and why else?" "Because we should take care of our things," said Kinzie. "Also true," Mom said kindly. "But the main reason we want you to make your beds each morning is to SHOW GRATITUDE for the bed you get to sleep in."

Luna frowned thoughtfully. "Can't we just SAY thank you?" she asked. "Yes," Mom agreed. "In fact, Dad and I start every morning by SAYING a prayer of thanks for our bed, too. But a more meaningful way to SHOW GRATITUDE is through ACTION - by SAYING a prayer *while* also MAKING our bed." "But why isn't praying enough?" Kinzie asked.

As she gently smoothed the sheets, Mom said, "Prayer is powerful. It's how we talk to God, share our worries, and say thank you for everything He does." She smiled and added, "But did you know that God also loves when we *do our part*?" Serenity tilted her head. "What do you mean?" she asked. "Praying without taking action is like asking someone to teach you how to tie your shoes, but then you never grab the laces to try it yourself," Mom explained. "When we **pray** and take **action**, it shows God we're ready to work with Him - and that's when amazing things start to happen."

"Do other people pray for their beds and make them each morning too?" Luna asked. "Not everyone has a safe and comfortable bed to sleep in like we do," Mom explained softly. "Many people, including children, sleep on hard floors without warm blankets or a soft pillow," she added. "In fact, some people sleep outside without the protection of a safe home."

Luna's eyes grew wide. "That makes me sad," she said softly. "It makes me sad too," Mom replied. "But SAYING a prayer *while* MAKING our bed is a simple way to mix **prayer** with **action** and a meaningful way to SHOW GRATITUDE for what we have and COMPASSION for those who have less," she added. "What's compassion?" asked Kinzie.

"Compassion is wanting to help others, especially those in need," Mom explained. "It's more than a feeling - it's taking action to show kindness," she added. "I think I'm understanding," Luna said slowly. "But I still don't know what WE can do to help people who don't have beds."

"Well, there are actually a lot of things we can do," Mom said. "For example, we can donate sheets and blankets to a local shelter, or we can donate money to an organization to help buy a bed for someone who doesn't have one," she added.

"But we're just kids!" exclaimed Serenity. "We don't have money to do that!" Mom smiled. "You may not have money, but there IS something you can ALL do to help," she said. "What is it?" Luna asked eagerly. "You can all take the Sleep Challenge," Mom announced.

"The Sleep Challenge?" repeated Kinzie. "Yes," said Mom. "It's when we give up our beds for one night and sleep on the floor - to understand what others experience." "How does that help?" Serenity wondered. "It helps us to understand what others experience and to care more deeply for them," Mom said. "And it's a great way to mix **prayer** with **action**, which will fill your hearts with GRATITUDE and COMPASSION."

"Let's do it tonight!" Luna exclaimed. "We can tell our friends, too!" Serenity added with excitement." "I love that idea," Mom said. "The more people who know, the more hearts we can open, and the more lives we can touch."

Together, the girls helped Mom finish making their beds. "Mom, will you say your prayer of thanks with us?" Luna asked. "Of course," Mom said warmly, "and I'll say it with you every day until you're ready to say it on your own."

As they finished the last bed, Mom prayed: "Dear Lord, thank you for the safe and comfortable bed that we get to sleep in when we need rest. We pray for those who don't have what we have. We ask that You provide them with safety and comfort, that You fill our hearts with gratitude and compassion, and that You show each of us how to use our blessings to love and serve others the way You want us to. Amen."

"Amen!" the girls echoed with smiles. "Now, let's go eat," Mom said.

With hearts full of GRATITUDE for what they have and COMPASSION for those who have less, the girls hurried back to the kitchen to share their plan with Dad and Micah - and to finish their yummy breakfast.

"Now that our bellies AND hearts are full," said Dad, "are we ready for our BIG day?"
"Yep, we're ready!" the kids cheered.

"Then let's go," said Mom, "because today is the day…"

"...Adoption Day!"

Message Inspiration

Growing up, my younger brother and I had daily chores; one of which was to make our beds every morning before we started our day. That simple routine stuck with me into adulthood and became second nature.

When my husband and I met, we, like many couples, had the classic "debate" about whether it was necessary to make our beds each day. After all, they would inevitably get messed up again when we crawled back into bed at the end of the day. Although I felt very strongly about making our beds each day, I couldn't convince him that it mattered - until I changed not just how I explained it, but how I viewed it myself.

For years, I viewed making my bed as a reflection of respect, responsibility, and self-discipline. However, that mindset transformed bed-making into a chore - something I *had* to do. Even for someone as optimistic as me, that perspective took the joy out of it.

When I shifted my perspective, I realized that making my bed each morning is LESS about responsibility and self-discipline (although still important and respectful) and MORE about **showing gratitude**. It's about recognizing the many small luxuries we too often take for granted, such as a safe place to rest, clean sheets, warmth, and comfort, and being grateful for those luxuries. It's also MORE about **showing compassion** for those who don't have those same blessings by combing **prayer** with **action**, as Jesus calls us to do.

Prayer is powerful - it's our way of talking to God, inviting His guidance into our lives, and putting all of our trust in Him. But here's the part we sometimes forget: God often answers our prayers by working *through* us. Praying without acting is like asking God to guide our path but never taking a step down it. When we add **action** to our **prayer**, we show God we're ready to work alongside Him. We join in the blessings we're asking for, and we're willing to do the work to see them come to life. When we **pray** and **take action,** we show faith in motion. It's seen in every choice we make. It's lived in every step we take. It's trusted in every move we make.

Prayers align our hearts with God's will. *Actions align our lives* with the path He's revealing. Together, they create the opportunity for God's purpose to unfold.

Once I started thinking of it that way, bed-making stopped feeling like a task and started feeling like a privilege - something I *wanted* to do, not something I *had* to do. That shift in perspective changed how I viewed bed-making, which then helped me convince my husband, and others, of its importance and impact in our lives.

As we make our bed, we say this simple prayer of thanks:
"Dear Lord, thank you for the safe and comfortable bed that we get to sleep in when we need rest. We pray for those who don't have what we have. We ask that You provide them with safety and comfort, that You fill our hearts with gratitude and compassion, and that You show each of us how to use our blessings and unique gifts to **love** and **serve** others the way YOU want us to. Amen."

This simple prayer transforms a simple act into a moment of peace to start our day. Too often, many of us wake up and immediately rush straight into the day, without taking a moment to align our minds and our hearts in a faith-driven direction. A simple **prayer** combined with a simple **action** can help us start our day with a foundation of gratitude and compassion to build upon throughout the day.

No matter where we are in life, whether we're content or wishing things were different in some way, we can always find ways to show **gratitude** for what we have and **compassion** for those who have less.

To develop a **heart of gratitude**, I invite you to take the **Gratitude Challenge**:
1. **Morning**: Start your day by making your bed while saying a **prayer of thanks**. Then, find three additional "luxuries" you're grateful for, such as a hot shower, a warm set of clothes, or a nutritious meal. Pray for those luxuries in your life and for those who don't have those same blessings.
2. **Throughout the day**: Notice and express gratitude for one person in your life. Every person we encounter can serve a purpose in our lives, even the more "challenging" ones.
3. **Before bed**: Reflect on your day and thank God for one challenge you faced. After all, our trials often hold the greatest opportunities for growth.

Embrace this routine for one week and observe how you feel. Maintain an open heart and mind, ready to see what might unfold. After the initial week, try two and then three. Remember, it only takes 21 days to establish a habit, and what better habit to cultivate than one of gratitude and thanksgiving. After all, it's more than a holiday once a year; it's one of the most important forms of worship. It not only honors God but also trains our hearts to recognize His care and provision in our lives every single day.

To foster a **heart of compassion**, we invite you to participate in the **Compassion Over Comfort Sleep Challenge**:
1. Simply forgo the comfort of your bed for a single night and sleep on the floor as a way to show compassion for those who don't have a bed to sleep in. May this simple gesture help us to put compassion over comfort.
2. Capture the gesture with a photo and share it on social media using the hashtag **#CompassionOverComfortSleepChallenge**.
3. If sleeping on the floor poses physical challenges, consider donating blankets to a local shelter or supporting organizations that provide beds for those in need, such as SHPbeds.org, BedBrigade.org, Beds4Vets.org, Down-Home.org, and more! A portion of our annual book sales goes directly to organizations like these.

www.ingramcontent.com/pod-product-compliance
Lightning Source LLC
LaVergne TN
LVHW070433070526
838199LV00014B/494